CONTIN PRIMARY SCHOOL

CONTIN PRIMARY SCHOOL

LIFE IN THE
RAINFORESTS

Written by **Lucy Baker**

Consultant Roger Hammond
Director of Living Earth

FRANKLIN WATTS
in association with
TWO-CAN

Rain Forests

First published in this edition in 1990 by
Franklin Watts
96 Leonard Street
London EC2A 4RH

© Two-Can Publishing Ltd, 1990

Text and Design Lucy Baker

Printed and bound in Hong Kong

A CIP Catalogue record of this book is available from the British Library

ISBN 0-7496-0322-4

Photographic Credits:
p.5 Bruce Coleman p.7 (top) Heather Angel/Biofotos (bottom) South American Pictures/Tony Morrison p.8 Bruce Coleman/E. & P. Bauer p.9 Ardea/Pat Morris p.10 (top) Ardea/
Anthony & Elizabeth Bomford (bottom) Bruce Coleman/J. Mackinnon p.11 (top) NHPA/L.H. Newman (centre) Survival Anglia/Claude Steelman (right) NHPA/Jany Sauvanet
p.12 (bottom) Ardea (top) Bruce Coleman p.13 Bruce Coleman p.14 The Hutchison Library/J. Von Puttkamer p.15 (top) Survival International/Steve Cox (bottom) The Hutchison
Library/J. Von Puttkamer p.16 Bruce Coleman/Michael Fogden p.17 Survival International/Victor Englebert p.18 Impact Photos p.19 The Hutchison Library p.20-21 NHPA p.22
Oxford Scientific Films/R.A. Acharya p.23 South American Pictures/Bill Leimbach p.31 Impact/Julio Eckhardt
Front cover: Front cover: Michael & Patricia Fogden Back cover: Tony Stone Worldwide

Illustrations by Francis Mosley. Story illustrated by Valerie McBride.

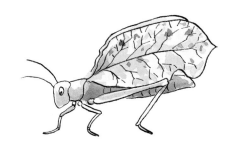

CONTENTS

LOOKING AT RAINFORESTS

Imagine a forest unchanged for 60 million years, where giant trees reach up to the sky, their leafy branches blocking out light to the forest floor below. Imagine a place where the temperature hardly changes from day to night, season to season, year to year. A place where rain clouds hang in the air and heavy downpours are common. The rainforest is such a place.

Inside the rainforest, as much as two-thirds of all land-based animals and plants can be found. Much of the remaining third of animal life probably originated from the rainforests thousands of years ago.

Rainforests are not only home to large numbers of animals and plants. People have lived in rainforests for generations.

DID YOU KNOW?

● Rainforests are the wettest areas of land in the world. As much as 10 m (over 32 feet) of rain may fall during a single year in some places.

● Almost half of the world's rainforests have been cut down in the last fifty years and the clearance continues. In 1989 rainforests were disappearing at a rate of 24 hectares (60 acres) every minute.

LAYERS OF THE RAINFOREST

Most rainforest life is found about 40 m (120 feet) above the ground, in the **canopy**. This is where the branches of the giant trees tangle together to form a lush, green platform.

Underneath the canopy, little can grow in the darkness. Where light does penetrate through the canopy, smaller trees and plants compete for space.

Little grows on the forest floor, but leaves and other debris rain down from the canopy. Plants, insects and animals convert this waste to food.

canopy

understorey

forest floor

WHERE IN THE WORLD

Over half of the world's rainforests are in South and Central America. The remainder can be found in parts of Africa, Asia and Australia. Almost all rainforests lie between two imaginary lines north and south of the **equator**, called the **Tropic of Cancer** and the **Tropic of Capricorn**. This is why they are often called tropical rainforests.

It has been hot and wet in the tropics for millions of years. These constant conditions have made it possible for rainforests to develop into the most diverse and complex **environments** in the world. Some scientists recognise over 40 different types of rainforest, each with its own variety of plant and animal life.

Rainforests once formed a wide, green belt around the planet but today pictures taken from space tell a different story. All around the world large areas of rainforest are vanishing as people clear the way for crops, homes and businesses. Many species of wildlife are disappearing too.

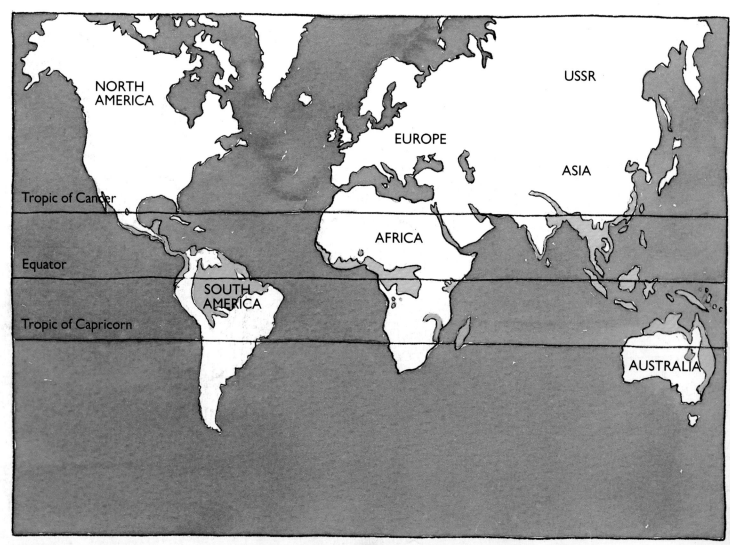

NORTH AMERICA

USSR

EUROPE

ASIA

Tropic of Cancer

AFRICA

Equator

SOUTH AMERICA

Tropic of Capricorn

AUSTRALIA

► In the tropics, the only change in weather conditions is from wet to wetter during the rainy season. This means that rainforest trees do not need to flower in spring or shed their leaves in autumn. Each type of tree has its own growth cycle. The varying tree cycles guarantee a regular supply of flowers, fruits, nuts and seeds for rainforest creatures.

▼ The largest rainforest in the world stretches across the Amazon Basin in South America. It covers an area nearly as big as Australia. The Amazon River snakes through the rainforest. It is the largest river system in the world. During the rainy season, parts of the rainforest are flooded by the Amazon and fish swim among the giant tree trunks.

THE PLANT BANK

Most of our woodlands are dominated by one type of tree such as oak or maple. In the rainforest, there can be over 80 species in a single acre of land.

Rainforests contain a huge variety of other plants too. Wherever light reaches the forest floor, an exotic layer of herbs and ferns flourish. Wiry stems hang like lifeless ropes around the giant tree trunks. These climbers and vines produce a mass of leaves and flowers in the canopy layer.

The canopy itself is like a huge aerial garden. Moss, lichen and hundreds of flowering plants cover the canopy branches. These plants, called **epiphytes**, do not harm the host tree. Their roots dangle in the air or grow in a thin layer of compost which forms in the dips and cracks of the many branches.

▲ The rafflesia grows on the forest floor in parts of Asia. It produces flowers up to 1m (3 feet) across – the biggest in the world. They have thick, warty petals and spiky centres that stink of rotting meat.

▶ Water and debris collect in some epiphytes and provide ponds for tiny rainforest frogs.

PLANT FACTS

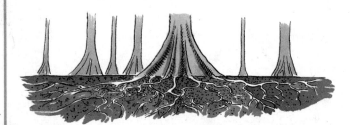

Rainforest trees have shallow root systems so they often produce special **buttress roots** to help keep themselves standing upright.

Most rainforest leaves are thick and waxy with special **drip-tips** to drain away water. They are often so big they can be used as umbrellas.

FEASTING IN THE FOREST

The lush vegetation of the rainforests is home to millions of different insects and other creepy crawlies. Some, like flies and beetles, act as cleaners, clearing the forest floor of waste and debris. Others, like wasps and bees, help to pollinate the flowers of the forest. Ants and spiders are also in abundance. Between them, they eat large numbers of other insects and so stop them becoming too plentiful.

The plants and insects of the rainforest provide thousands of different animals with food to eat. Here are some of the animals that can be found feasting in the forests.

▲ Lizards can be found all over the rainforest, eating insects, plants and, occasionally, small animals. Most lizards seize insects in their mouths, but a few snatch them from the air with their extra-long tongues.

◄ The giant, red orang-utans have huge appetites. They love to eat fruit, but they will also chew leaves, shoots and tree bark and, occasionally, take eggs from birds' nests. To help them find their favourite fruit, the clever orang-utans watch the birds that share their tastes in food and follow them through the forest. Orang-utans spend most of their lives in the treetops, swinging from branch to branch. Their long, powerful arms and hook-shaped hands make treetop climbing easy work. Orang-utans can be found in the rainforests of Borneo and Sumatra in South-East Asia.

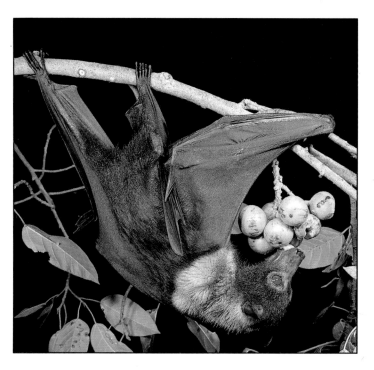

▲ Bats are commonplace in the rainforests. They are not birds, but the world's only flying mammals. Many bats hunt insects but some, like the flying fox shown here, eat fruit. Fruit bats help to spread seeds around the forest.

▲ The hummingbird's long, thin bill is ideal for getting to the sweet nectar found inside flowers, but these birds also eat insects. Hummingbirds are flying experts and can even fly backwards.

▶ Sloths have strict leaf-eating diets. They spend practically all their time in the treetops. There are two-toed sloths and three-toed sloths, like the one in this picture. Algae, beetles, moths and mites hide in the sloth's hair.

FOREST FIENDS

The rainforest is a dangerous place. The brightly-coloured parrots, chattering monkeys and slumbering sloths may seem carefree but they have their enemies. When a giant eagle soars overhead or an agile cat is on the prowl, the whole canopy is gripped in terror.

Big cats and eagles are the largest hunters in the forest, but there are hundreds of others. In the canopy, long, slender tree-snakes catch lizards, frogs and small birds. On the forest floor, huge, heavy constrictors, like the anaconda, wait for larger prey, such as wild boar or deer that forage in the leaf litter.

Small creatures can pose a greater threat to life. Scorpions, spiders, bees and wasps are found all over the forest. Many have poisonous bites or stings that can cause rashes, sickness or even death.

▲ Each rainforest has its own type of giant eagle. In Africa it is the crowned eagle, in South America the harpy eagle, and in Asia the monkey-eating eagle shown here. Giant eagles catch monkeys, sloths and other large prey in the canopy layer.

◄ Some forest cats, like margays and clouded leopards, are excellent tree climbers. They will chase monkeys and squirrels through the **understorey**. Others, like this jaguar, prefer to wait quietly on low, overhanging branches and pounce on animals as they pass beneath them.

◄ The bushmaster hunts small animals that scavenge on the forest floor. It is a venomous snake which means that it injects poison when it bites. The bushmaster is one of the most feared snakes in South America. Its bite can kill a person within hours. Luckily this snake is shy and is not often seen!

PROTECTION FROM PERIL

The smallest rainforest creatures have the greatest number of natural enemies so it is not surprising that they have developed many ways to defend themselves.

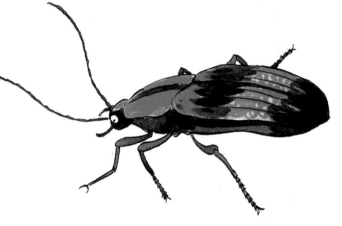

Some rainforest creatures produce a poison in their bodies which makes them unpleasant to eat. Bold markings advertise the fact and predators learn to recognise the warning markings.

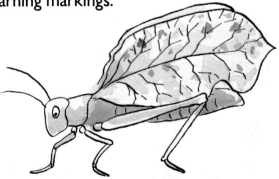

Some butterflies have hidden eyespots on their wings which are flashed at would-be predators. The false eyes startle the attackers and this gives the butterflies a chance to escape.

To reduce the risk of being eaten, many insects have clever **camouflage**, like this bush cricket.

RAINFOREST PEOPLE

Modern people are uncomfortable in the rainforest. They find the hot, humid conditions stifling. Every step they take is fraught with danger and, although there is food all around them, they cannot tell a poisonous berry from a nutritious and refreshing fruit.

Certain groups of people have lived in the rainforests for thousands of years. To them, the rainforest is home and the only world they know. Rainforest tribes live in structured communities with their own cultures and customs. They have a very deep understanding of the way the rainforests work. They know which plants and animals are useful and how to take from the forest without harm.

There are rainforest tribes in parts of Africa, Asia and South America, but their way of life is threatened. Although they have rights according to international laws, they are often mistreated and their land is stolen or invaded. If all the ancient tribes disappear, their detailed knowledge of the rainforest may be lost forever.

▼ A large area of rainforest can support only a few hundred people, so rainforest tribes are spread thinly through the wooded lands. Some tribes build communal houses, where many families live together.

◀ Rainforest children do not have to go to school, but they still have a lot to learn. Their elders must teach them everything there is to know about life in the rainforest.

▼ Many rainforest people paint their bodies with colourful dyes and use feathers, flowers and other natural materials to make simple pieces of jewellery.

PEOPLE FACTS

The Pygmy people of the African rainforest are very small. The tallest of them are only some 1.4m (four feet eight inches) tall.

Life is not easy in the rainforest. A person in the modern world may live for over 70 years. In the rainforest, few people survive more than 40 years. Diseases, like flu and measles, introduced by European settlers, are still big killers of native tribes. Over 80 different tribes have died out in Brazil since 1900.

GIFTS FROM THE FOREST

Rainforest **tribes** can get everything they need from their homeland. The many different plants and animals found in the forest provide the raw materials for meals, houses, clothes, medicines, tools and cosmetics.

We also use rainforest products. Many of the fruits, nuts and cereals that fill our supermarket shelves originated in the rainforest. The domestic chicken, which is now farmed worldwide, began life on the forest floor. The most expensive **hardwoods**, like teak, mahogany and ebony, come from rainforest trees.

Other rainforest products include tea, coffee, cocoa, rubber and many types of medicine.

We still know very little about the rainforests. Scientists believe there are thousands of future foodstuffs, medicines and other raw materials waiting to be discovered.

▼ These tiny rainforest frogs produce a strong poison under their skin to stop other animals from eating them. Some tribes extract this poison by gently roasting the frogs and collecting their sweat. They use it to tip their blow-pipe darts when they hunt big game.

RAINFOREST TREASURES

There is an Amazonian tree that produces a sap very similar to diesel. It can be poured straight into a truck's tank and used as fuel.

A quarter of all medicines owe their origins to rainforest plants and animals.

Rainforest insects could offer an alternative to expensive pesticides. In Florida, three kinds of wasp were successfully introduced to control pests that were damaging the citrus tree crops.

There are at least 1500 potential new fruits and vegetables growing in the world's rainforests.

▲ A hunter from the Yanomami tribe hunts monkeys and other game, while women and children search the forest floor for food.

RAINFOREST DESTRUCTION

Rainforests are natural treasure-houses but they are being destroyed for nothing more than timber and the land on which they stand. This is because most rainforests are found in poor, developing countries. These countries cannot afford to keep their beautiful forests.

Large areas of rainforest are sold to timber companies. They send bulldozers and chainsaw gangs into the forest to cut down the hardwood trees. The wildlife flees and, although only the oldest and largest trees are felled, over half of the forest may be damaged by the time all the work is finished.

Rainforests are cleared completely to reach rich mineral reserves, such as iron, copper or uranium, or to make huge cash-crop plantations of coffee, cocoa or bananas.

Big business is only half the story. There are thousands of poor, homeless people in rainforest countries who are encouraged to leave the overcrowded cities and farm pieces of rainforest land. They are called **slash and burn** farmers because they build simple homesteads in the forest and then burn the surrounding vegetation to enrich the soil.

▼ An estimated 500 million people have moved into the world's rainforests and more are sure to follow. They clear the forest to farm small areas of land for food and money.

DID YOU KNOW?

● Industrial countries buy over 18 times more hardwood today than they did 50 years ago.

● Over half of Central America's rainforests have gone. They have been cleared to build huge cattle ranches. Much of the meat produced is sold to western countries to feed the demands of their growing burger market.

▶ See the difference between the rich world of the distant green rainforest and the lifeless cracked earth in the foreground. Huge areas of Brazil have been devastated and animals and plants are gone forever.

PARADISE LOST

It can take less than ten years for rainforest land to become as barren and lifeless as a desert. This is because most rainforests are found on poor clay soils. Only a thin layer of nutritious topsoil covers the forest floor and this is anchored down by giant tree trunks.

Slash and burn farmers clear rainforest land to grow their crops. But after only a few years, the tropical rains wash the **topsoil** away and the land becomes too difficult to cultivate.

FROM GOOD TO BAD

Trees and plants help to keep the air around us clean. They use sunlight, water and air to make food. In the food-making process, they make use of the part of the air that we breathe out (carbon dioxide) and produce the part that we breathe in (oxygen).

When rainforests are burnt down to clear land, the trees stop using up carbon dioxide. Instead, the forest fires produce carbon dioxide which pollutes the atmosphere.

The wastelands left behind by farmers are baked by the sun and drenched by the rains. The rains, which would have watered thirsty trees and plants, fall straight to the ground and run downhill, carrying tons of soil with them. Valleys are flooded and freshwater rivers become clogged up with mud.

Tropical scientists believe that, at the present rate of destruction, there will be no rainforests left by the year 2050. If this paradise is lost, thousands of different plants and animals will disappear for ever.

SAVE THE RAINFORESTS

More and more people are becoming aware of the need to save the rainforests. Some steps have already been taken to slow down the rate of destruction. Native tribes have blocked the path of bulldozers and chainsaw gangs and many **conservation** groups have launched huge rainforest campaigns.

Much more could still be done to save the world's rainforests. Timber companies could change the way they harvest the forest, to reduce the amount of damage they cause. They could also be made to replant areas of forest that have been disturbed. Slash and burn farmers could be taught better ways to farm rainforest lands. By planting trees and crops together, they could preserve the fragile topsoil and use the same piece of land for many years.

Rich, industrial countries could help too. Rainforest countries are using up their beautiful forests to pay off huge debts to western countries. If these debts were reduced, more money could be spent on developing the cleared land and the remaining forests could be preserved.

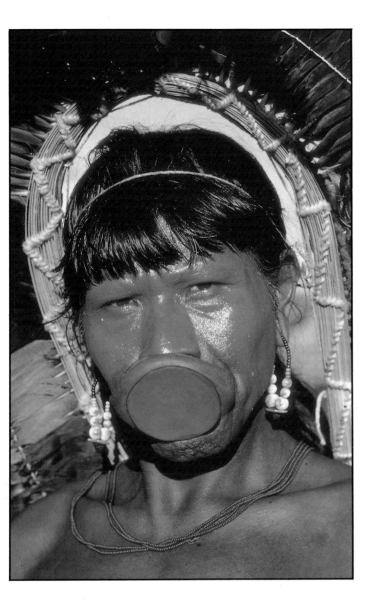

▲ Raoni is a chief of the Kayapo Indians in Brazil. He has travelled thousands of kilometers from his rainforest home to speak about the problems his people face. Their land has been invaded by foresters and slash and burn farmers. The forests, which they rely upon for food and shelter, are being destroyed.

◀ Scientists believe that over 50 wild species of insects, plants and animals become extinct every day because of rainforest destruction. Many of the world's favourite animals, like tigers and orang-utans, are endangered because their rainforest homes are being destroyed. By protecting large areas of rainforest, these animals could be saved from **extinction**.

RAINFOREST ACTION

Spread the word
Tell your friends and relatives about the plight of the rainforests. Write to the government and ask them to help rainforest countries.

Support rainforest campaigns
There are many charities and pressure groups trying to slow down the rate of rainforest destruction. They need money and support to continue their work. Watch out for news of how you can help them on television, the radio or in newspapers and magazines.

THE COWRIE THIEVES

For thousands of years people have told stories about the world around them. Often these stories try to explain something that people do not really understand, like how the world began, or where light comes from. This tale is told by the people of the Congo in Africa.

Long ago, in a village right in the middle of the Congo, there lived a man and his wife who were always causing mischief.

All the other villagers agreed that these two had the most irritating habits. They hardly ever did any work, preferring to sit around and chatter to one another. When they did start to work, they would tire of whatever they were doing very quickly and wander off to do something else.

They were always dropping in at their neighbours' huts, just when dinner was ready. Their neighbours were obliged to ask them in to supper, that being the custom.

But the worst thing of all was the way they would pick up other people's belongings. The two of them would just wander into other people's huts and start picking up anything that they could see. They would poke their noses into baskets, take a mouthful of food or just move everything around so that the owner of the hut would come home to a terrible mess.

The other villagers put up with the pair because they never really did much harm. Whenever a villager lost his temper with them, they looked so hurt at the thought that they had done wrong and promised so fervently to mend their ways that it was impossible to be angry for long.

One day, however, they wandered into the hut of an important man in the village and pulled out his bag of cowrie shells, all his wealth, from under his bed. They tipped the cowrie shells out over the floor and began to play with them, counting them, rolling them around and making patterns on the floor.

Eventually the mischievous man decided to go and find some food, and his mischievous wife followed him, leaving the cowrie shells scattered all over the floor.

When the owner of the hut came back and saw his cowrie shells scattered about, his first thought was that he had been robbed.

He shouted to all the other villagers to come and see what had happened. The woman from the hut next door said that she had seen the mischievous man and his mischievous wife coming out of the important man's hut.

Just then, someone spotted the mischievous man and his mischievous wife coming around the corner with a bunch of bananas. They looked very surprised when they were accused of stealing the cowrie shells.

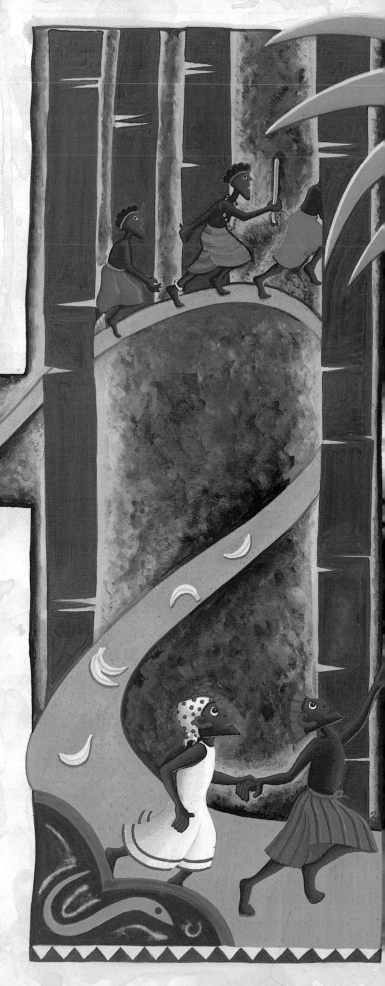

The important man who thought he had been robbed did not wait for an explanation. "Just you wait until I get you!..." he yelled.

He rushed at the pair waving his arms fiercely. The mischievous man and his mischievous wife ran as fast as they could into the shelter of the forest, with all the villagers rushing after them.

When they reached the forest, the mischievous man and his mischievous wife climbed up a tree to hide from the villagers. For a few minutes the villagers chasing them were puzzled. Then one of them spotted the mischievous wife's hair hanging down from a branch.

"Let's sit up here and wait until they go away, and then go down," said the mischievous man.

But the villagers didn't go away. The important man who thought that he had been robbed stood at the bottom of the tree and shouted: "Don't think you'll get away with it that easily!"

The villagers set a guard by the bottom of the tree, waiting for the mischievous man and his wife to come down.

Time passed, and the villagers guarding the bottom of the tree changed twice a day, until all of them had guarded the tree once. The mischievous man and his mischievous wife sat in the tree, chattering to one another, and pulling off fruit from the nearby branches. Their fingers and toes began to get very long and thin from gripping the branches and stretching out for fruit.

One day, when all the villagers had guarded the bottom of the tree twice, the mischievous man and his mischievous wife realised that the hair on their bodies had grown long and thick, making it hard for them to be seen in the branches.

One day, when all the villagers had guarded the bottom of the tree three times, the mischievous man and his mischievous wife felt a funny sensation at the bottom of their spines. They had grown tails! They jumped up and down on their branch, chattering to one another very fast, and swinging with their new tails.

And that is why, even though the people of the Congo are often annoyed with mischievous monkeys who come into their houses and make a mess or take their food, they never harm them.

The villager at the bottom of the tree, heard all the noise and stared up at the pair. What a surprise he got! The mischievous man and his mischievous wife had turned into monkeys!

When the villager went back to the village, to tell the others what he had seen, the important man who thought he had been robbed was furious. But later, when he had counted his cowrie shells, he realised how unjust he had been. How he regretted his hastiness!

TRUE OR FALSE?

Which of these facts are true and which ones are false? If you have read this book carefully, you will know the answers.

1. Rainforests are found all over Europe.

2. Rainforests lie between the Tropics of Capricorn and Cancer.

3. There are up to 40 kinds of rainforest.

4. Orang-utans are found in the forests of Africa.

5. Over 80 tree species grow in one acre of rainforest.

6. The world's largest rainforest is in Australia.

7. Algae and insects shelter in the long fur of the sloth.

8. Giant eagles feed on animals from the forest floor.

9. Chickens originally came from the rainforest.

10. Tribespeople collect poison from rainforest frogs by squeezing them.

11. Sap from a tree in the Amazon basin can be used as diesel fuel in trucks.

12. Slash and burn farming helps the soil to grow richer.

13. The rainforests may be destroyed by the year 2050.

ANSWERS: 1. False 2. True 3. True 4. False 5. True 6. False 7. True 8. False 9. True 10. False 11. True 12. False 13. True

GLOSSARY

● **Buttress roots** develop to support the heavy trunks and help keep the tall trees of the rainforest upright.

● **Camouflage** is the method by which the surface of certain creatures is covered in patterns or colours matching their background. These help to hide them from predators. A chameleon can change its body colour according to the background it walks against.

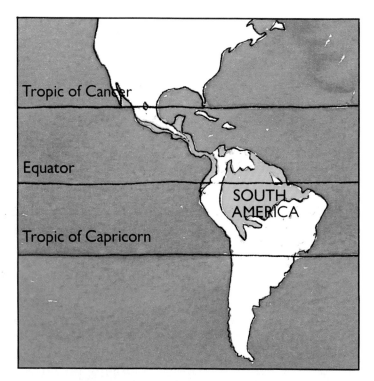

● **Canopy** is the uppermost layer of the rainforest, the dense leafy section some 6–7 m (18–21 feet) deep, at 40-50 m (120–150 feet) above ground.

● **Conservation** is the preservation of natural species and environments from excessive exploitation by humans. This involves help from governments and scientists.

● **Drip-tip** is the long tip on most leaves in the rainforest, developed to shed rain from the leaf's waxy surface.

● **Environment** is the particular combination of conditions in an area, which affects the type of living things inhabiting it.

● **Epiphyte** is a plant growing on another plant without damaging it. It is not a parasite.

● **Equator** is the imaginary line exactly halfway between North and South Poles.

● **Extinction** occurs when the last member of an animal or plant species dies out after overhunting, a change in its habitat or failure to compete with a new arrival in its niche.

● **Hardwood** trees such as ebony, teak and mahogany grow in the rainforest. Their tough wood is excellent for making strong furniture and this is one cause of the destruction of large parts of the rainforest.

● **Scavenger** is a creature which feeds on the refuse left by others, for instance, on another animal's kill.

● **Tropic of Cancer, Tropic of Capricorn** are imaginary lines at about 23°27″ north and south of the equator, at the point where the sun changes its course over the earth's surface. The area between these two lines is known as the Tropics and most rainforests are found in this region.

● **Understorey** is the name for the smaller trees and bushes which make up the middle level in a rainforest, below the tops of the taller trees.

● **Slash and burn** farming is practised by poor farmers who clear areas of the rainforest for soil on which to grow their crops. These farmers move on every few seasons as the soil holds little good once the trees have gone.

● **Topsoil** lies above the stony ground beneath the rainforest floor. This rich earth is held in place by the trees but is rapidly washed away by rains when they are cut down.

● **Tribe** is a community of people who live together for protection from danger and for a shared way of life.

INDEX